this
JOURNAL
belongs to

_____

_____

LOVE GOD GREATLY

Journal

Love God Greatly Bible Journal

Copyright © 2020 by Love God Greatly

Published in Nashville, TN, by HarperCollins Christian Publishing, Inc.

Thomas Nelson is a registered trademark of HarperCollins Christian Publishing, Inc.

Scripture quotations are taken from The NET Bible, New English Translation. Copyright © 1996, 2019 by Biblical Studies Press, LLC.

ISBN: 9780785239062

Library of Congress Cataloging-in-Publication Data

All rights reserved. No portion of this book may be reproduced, stored in a retrieval system, or transmitted in any form or by any means—electronic, mechanical, photocopy, recording, or any other—except for brief quotation in printed reviews, without the prior permission of the publisher.

Printed in South Korea

20 21 22 23 24 25 /SWK/ 6 5 4 3 2 1

**MORE THAN SIXTY-ONE PERCENT
OF WOMEN WORLDWIDE DO
NOT HAVE ACCESS TO BIBLICAL
MATERIALS OR CHRISTIAN
COMMUNITIES.**

At Love God Greatly we create resources
to bring God's Word to women in every
community, in every nation, in every
language so they can love God greatly
with their lives.

Welcome, Friend!

We're so glad you're here.

Join Us

ONLINE
lovegodgreatly.com

STORE
lovegodgreatly.com/store

FACEBOOK
facebook.com/LoveGodGreatly

INSTAGRAM
instagram.com/lovegodgreatlyofficial

TWITTER
twitter.com/_lovegodgreatly

DOWNLOAD THE APP

CONTACT US
info@lovegodgreatly.com

CONNECT
#LoveGodGreatly

Contents

WHAT IS LOVE GOD GREATLY?

Love God Greatly (LGG) is an international women's ministry that exists to inspire, encourage, and equip women to love God greatly with their lives by breaking down the barriers that exist around studying God's Word. We provide free, quality Bible study resources to women in twenty-four languages. Through online and in-person groups, women in more than two hundred countries read and study God's Word and grow in community together.

Our heart is to be people who love God with our whole selves and our whole lives every day. We've found that the best way to love Him greatly is to study His Word and be in community with His people.

We've designed this journal to help you do just that. In it you'll find lots of space to study God's Word and record what you're learning. You can use this journal with the *Love God Greatly Bible*, recording your reading plans and working through the SOAP method. We hope this journal becomes a place for you to engage with Scripture and record what God is teaching you.

---

*Our heart is to be people who love God with our whole selves
and our whole lives every day.*

In this journal you'll find pages to fill in your Scripture reading for the day and space to write down observations, applications, and prayers. You'll also find additional resources in both the front and back of this journal to help you as you study God's Word. We've included some brief instructions and tips to help you use the SOAP method of Bible study and reflection questions that can be applied to any passage you study. You will also find a few reading plans to get you started. You can find more reading plans in the *Love God Greatly Bible* or at LoveGodGreatly.com.

So grab a friend, a coworker, a neighbor, or a family member, choose a reading plan, and get started! We are thankful for your partnership as we seek to further the gospel and make God's Word available to every woman, in every community, in every nation.

THE *Lord* IS
slow to anger
& ABOUNDING
in loyal love

GLOBAL PURSUITS

Love God Greatly (LGG) provides free, quality Bible study resources for women. Through online and in-person groups, women in more than two hundred countries read and study God's Word and grow in community together.

Our Bible studies are packed with resources to help women grow in their walks with God. We include reading plans, reflection questions, devotionals, blog posts, and training in Bible study methods to inspire, encourage, and equip women.

Each Bible study is translated into twenty-four different languages and made available for free to women all over the world. We also offer companion Bible studies for kids, enabling women to engage in Bible study with their children.

Each Bible study is translated into twenty-four different languages and made available for free to women all over the world.

Women can find small groups to participate in for each Bible study via online or in-person communities. These groups are led by trained facilitators who continue our mission of inspiring, encouraging, and equipping women to love God greatly with their lives.

Love God Greatly is a 501(c)(3), nonprofit, organization. Funding for Love God Greatly comes through generous donations and proceeds from our online Bible study journals and books.

Love God Greatly is committed to providing quality Bible study materials and believes finances should never get in the way of a woman being able to participate in one of our studies. All journals are available to download for free from LoveGodGreatly.com. One hundred percent of proceeds are reinvested into Love God Greatly to help us continue to provide women all over the world with God's Word.

GOD LOVES YOU.

God's Word says, "For this is the way God loved the world: He gave his one and only Son, so that everyone who believes in him will not perish but have eternal life" (John 3:16).

OUR SIN SEPARATES US FROM GOD.

We are all sinners by nature and by choice, and because of this we are separated from God, who is holy. God's Word says, "For all have sinned and fall short of the glory of God" (Rom 3:23).

JESUS DIED SO THAT YOU MIGHT HAVE LIFE.

The consequence of sin is death, but God's free gift of salvation is available to us. Jesus took the penalty for our sin when He died on the cross. God's Word says, "For the payoff of sin is death, but the gift of God is eternal life in Christ Jesus our Lord" (Rom 6:23); "But God demonstrates his own love for us, in that while we were still sinners, Christ died for us" (Rom 5:8).

JESUS LIVES!

Death could not hold Him, and three days after His body was placed in the tomb Jesus rose again, defeating sin and death forever. He lives today in heaven and is preparing a place in eternity for all who believe in Him. Jesus said, "There are many dwelling places in my Father's house. Otherwise, I would have told you, because I am going away to make ready a place for you. And if I go and make ready a place for you, I will come again and take you to be with me, so that where I am you may be too" (John 14:2–3).

YOU CAN KNOW THAT YOU ARE FORGIVEN.

Accepting Jesus as your Savior is not about what you can do. Rather, it's having faith in Jesus and what He has already done. It takes recognizing that you are a sinner, believing that Jesus lived a sinless life because it pleased the Father and was willing to die at the hands of sinful man to atone for your sins, and asking for forgiveness by placing your full trust in His finished work on the cross on your behalf. God's Word says, "If you confess with your mouth that Jesus is Lord and believe in your heart that God raised him from the dead, you will be saved. For with the heart one believes and thus has righteousness and with the mouth one confesses and thus has salvation" (Rom 10:9–10).

SOAP

WHAT IS SOAP?

The Word of God is living and active. The words of Scripture are powerful, effective, and relevant for life at all times and in all cultures.

At Love God Greatly, we use the SOAP Bible study method. The acronym stands for Scripture, Observation, Application, and Prayer. When we intentionally slow down to reflect on Scripture, its truths start jumping off the page. The SOAP method allows us to dig deeper into God's Word and see more than we would if we simply read verses. We're better equipped to live out the message God's Word carries and not merely listen to it (see Jas 1:22).

In all of our reading plans, we read a passage of Scripture and then apply the SOAP method to a few verses. We believe that using this method allows us to glean a greater understanding of Scripture, which allows us to apply it effectively to our lives.

The most important ingredients in the SOAP method are your interaction with God's Word and the application of it to your life. God's Word is powerful and effective. You will never waste time in God's Word. Take time to study it carefully, discovering the truth of God's character and heart for the world.

THE SOAP METHOD INCLUDES FOUR STEPS:

SCRIPTURE
Write out the verses. Slow down and copy the passage from the text, focusing on what you are writing. Writing it more than one time is always helpful.

OBSERVATION
Take time to observe the passage carefully. What do you see in the verses you're reading? Who is the intended audience? To whom is the writer speaking? What cultural factors are at play? Are any words or themes repeated? What literary devices are used?

APPLICATION
After carefully observing what is happening in the passage, determine the main message or truth in the passage. How can you apply this truth to your life?

PRAYER
Pray God's Word back to Him. If He has revealed something to you during this time, pray about it. Confess any sin God has revealed. Pray through the truth of the passage.

S

STANDS FOR
SCRIPTURE

Physically write out the
SOAP verses. You'll be
amazed at what God will
reveal to you when you
just take the time to slow
down and write out what
you are reading!

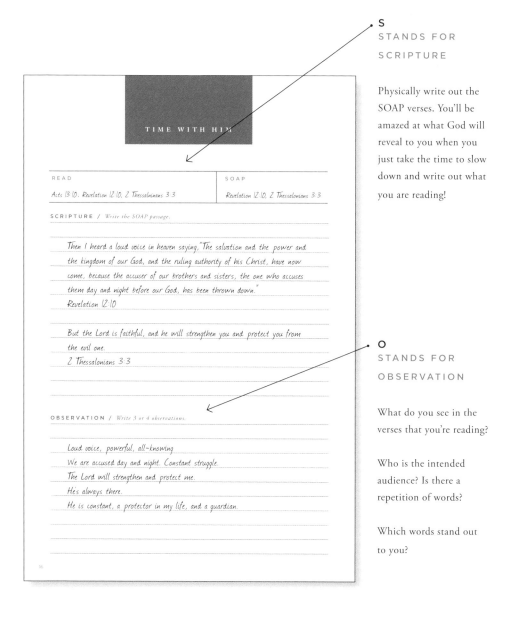

TIME WITH HIM

READ

Acts 13:10, Revelation 12:10, 2 Thessalonians 3:3

SOAP

Revelation 12:10, 2 Thessalonians 3:3

SCRIPTURE / Write the SOAP passage.

Then I heard a loud voice in heaven saying, "The salvation and the power and
the kingdom of our God, and the ruling authority of his Christ, have now
come, because the accuser of our brothers and sisters, the one who accuses
them day and night before our God, has been thrown down."
Revelation 12:10

But the Lord is faithful, and he will strengthen you and protect you from
the evil one.
2 Thessalonians 3:3

OBSERVATION / Write 3 or 4 observations.

Loud voice, powerful, all-knowing
We are accused day and night. Constant struggle.
The Lord will strengthen and protect me.
He's always there.
He is constant, a protector in my life, and a guardian.

O

STANDS FOR
OBSERVATION

What do you see in the
verses that you're reading?

Who is the intended
audience? Is there a
repetition of words?

Which words stand out
to you?

STANDS FOR APPLICATION

This is when God's Word becomes personal.

What is God saying to you today? How can you apply what you just read to your own life?

What changes do you need to make? Is there action you need to take?

APPLICATION / *Write 1 or 2 applications.*

Remind myself that God's strength is more powerful than anything.
Memorize these verses and say them daily this week.
Ask God to strengthen my faith in Him.
Trust that God will deliver me from evil.
Pray for my brothers and sisters in Christ.

PRAYER / *Write a prayer over what you learned.*

Dear Lord,

Thank You for being constant, faithful, and loving to me. Help me to put
my trust and faith in you daily and in the difficult times.

Help me to know You're always there by my side, strengthening and
protecting me. Remind me of the suffering of others and enable me to
comfort and encourage them in their growth.

I ask all these things in Jesus' name, amen.

17

P

STANDS FOR PRAYER

Pray God's Word back to Him. Spend time thanking Him.
If He has revealed something to you during this time in His Word, pray about it. If He
has revealed sin in your life, confess it. And remember, He loves you greatly.

WHAT I AM COMMANDING you today is to love THE LORD your GOD TO WALK IN His ways and to OBEY His COMMANDMENTS, His Statutes, and His ordinances

FEAR AND ANXIETY / SIX-WEEK STUDY

	MONDAY	TUESDAY	WEDNESDAY	THURSDAY	FRIDAY
1	Jeremiah 29:11 Romans 8:28 Revelation 1:17–18 SOAP Jeremiah 29:11	Proverbs 1:33 Proverbs 3:25–26 Luke 6:46–49 SOAP Proverbs 1:33	Proverbs 29:25 Isaiah 51:7 SOAP Proverbs 29:25	Psalm 68:5 Isaiah 41:10 SOAP Isaiah 41:10	Luke 12:22–26 John 16:33 SOAP Luke 12:22
2	Mark 4:40 Luke 8:22–25 SOAP Luke 8:25	Psalm 55:4–5 Psalm 94:19 SOAP Psalm 94:19	Isaiah 54:17 John 10:10 1 Peter 5:8–9 SOAP Isaiah 54:17	Romans 8:1–4 SOAP Romans 8:1	Psalm 34:11–14 Proverbs 3:7–8 Proverbs 14:26–27 SOAP Proverbs 3:7–8
3	Luke 12:22–31 John 10:27–29 SOAP John 10:29	Psalm 91:1–16 Colossians 1:13–14 SOAP Colossians 1:13–14	Zephaniah 3:17 Romans 8:31–39 1 John 4:18–19 SOAP Romans 8:37–39	Job 26:7–14 Matthew 28:18 SOAP Matthew 28:18	Psalm 27:1–3 SOAP Psalm 27:1
4	Romans 12:2 2 Corinthians 10:3–5 SOAP 2 Corinthians 10:5	Mark 5:35 Colossians 3:2 2 Timothy 1:7 SOAP Colossians 3:2	Deuteronomy 31:6 Psalm 23:4 SOAP Deuteronomy 31:6	Psalm 34:4 Psalm 118:5–7 John 17:9–19 SOAP Psalm 118:5–7	Isaiah 41:13–14 Isaiah 43:1–2 SOAP Isaiah 43:1–2
5	Acts 16:25–26 Philippians 4:4–8 1 Thessalonians 5:16 SOAP Philippians 4:4	Isaiah 40:29–31 Philippians 4:19 Hebrews 10:19–23 SOAP Philippians 4:19	Psalm 69:30 Colossians 3:17 1 Thessalonians 5:18 SOAP Colossians 3:17	Philippians 4:6–7 1 Thessalonians 5:17 SOAP Philippians 4:6	Proverbs 15:4 Matthew 15:11 Ephesians 4:25–32 SOAP Proverbs 15:4
6	Psalm 119:105 Ephesians 6:10–18 SOAP Ephesians 6:11–12	Proverbs 16:3 SOAP Proverbs 16:3	Romans 12:21 SOAP Romans 12:21	Philippians 4:9 James 1:22–25 SOAP James 1:22–23	Proverbs 3:5–8 Romans 16:20 SOAP Proverbs 3:5–8

DRAW NEAR / SIX-WEEK STUDY

	MONDAY	TUESDAY	WEDNESDAY	THURSDAY	FRIDAY
1	Psalm 19:1-3 Psalm 33:6-9 SOAP Psalm 19:1-3	Job 12:7-10 John 1:1-3 SOAP John 1:1-3	Psalm 19:1-3 Psalm 96:10-13 SOAP Psalm 96:10-13	Job 38:4-5 Psalm 95 SOAP Job 38:4-5	Psalm 19:1-3 Psalm 104:24-25 SOAP Psalm 104:24-25
2	Psalm 19:4-6 Colossians 2:1-10 SOAP Psalm 19:4-6	Romans 1:18-21 1 Timothy 2:3-4 SOAP Romans 1:20	Psalm 19:4-6 John 1:14-18 SOAP John 1:14	Jeremiah 29:12-14 James 4:8 SOAP James 4:8	Psalm 19:4-6 Colossians 1:15-20 SOAP Colossians 1:15-16
3	Psalm 19:7-9 Jeremiah 15:16 SOAP Psalm 19:7-9	2 Timothy 3:16-17 2 Peter 1:20-21 SOAP 2 Timothy 3:16-17	Psalm 19:7-9 Isaiah 55:8-13 SOAP Isaiah 55:8-11	Proverbs 30:5-6 Hebrews 4:12-13 SOAP Proverbs 30:5-6	Psalm 19:7-9 Matthew 24:35 SOAP Matthew 24:35
4	Psalm 19:10-11 John 17:14-19 SOAP Psalm 19:10-11	Psalm 119:17-18 Luke 11:28 SOAP Psalm 119:17-18	Psalm 19:10-11 Matthew 4:1-4 SOAP Matthew 4:4	Psalm 33:4 Ephesians 6:14-18 SOAP Ephesians 6:14-18	Psalm 19:10-11 Colossians 3:16-17 SOAP Colossians 3:16-17
5	Psalm 1:1-2 Psalm 19:12-13 SOAP Psalm 19:12-13	Psalm 119:105 1 Peter 1:22-23 SOAP 1 Peter 1:22-23	Psalm 19:12-13 James 1:19-27 SOAP James 1:25	Romans 15:1-5 2 Timothy 2:1-2 SOAP Romans 15:4	Psalm 19:12-13 Psalm 119:9-16 SOAP Psalm 119:11
6	Psalm 19:14 2 Timothy 2:14-19 SOAP Psalm 19:14	Deuteronomy 11:16-25 Joshua 1:7-9 SOAP Joshua 1:8	Psalm 19:14 Romans 10:5-17 SOAP Romans 10:17	Colossians 1:3-8 1 Thessalonians 2:9-16 SOAP 1 Thessalonians 2:13	Psalm 19:14 Philippians 1:3-11 SOAP Philippians 1:6

TRUTH OVER LIES / SIX-WEEK STUDY

	MONDAY	TUESDAY	WEDNESDAY	THURSDAY	FRIDAY
1	Genesis 3:1-4 John 8:44 Ephesians 6:11 SOAP John 8:44 Ephesians 6:11	Acts 13:10 2 Thessalonians 3:3 Revelation 12:10 SOAP 2 Thessalonians 3:3 Revelation 12:10	Jeremiah 17:9-10 Ezekiel 36:26 1 Corinthians 3:18 SOAP Jeremiah 17:9-10	Colossians 2:8 2 Timothy 3:13-14 1 John 2:15-16 1 John 5:19 SOAP Colossians 2:8	Psalm 119:11 Acts 17:11 1 Thessalonians 5:21 1 John 4:1 SOAP Psalm 119:11
2	Ephesians 2:8 1 John 4:19 SOAP Ephesians 2:8	Psalm 73:23-26 2 Corinthians 12:9 Philippians 4:19 SOAP 2 Corinthians 12:9 Philippians 4:19	Isaiah 54:4-5 Romans 8:1 SOAP Romans 8:1	John 1:16 Romans 8:31-32 Ephesians 1:3-8 James 1:5 SOAP Romans 8:31-32	Isaiah 43:25 1 John 1:9 SOAP Isaiah 43:25 1 John 1:9
3	Exodus 4:1-11 Ephesians 2:10 Philippians 4:13 1 Peter 2:9 SOAP Exodus 4:11	Hebrews 13:20-21 Philippians 4:13 SOAP Hebrews 13:20-21	Romans 5:8 Romans 8:37-39 SOAP Romans 5:8	Proverbs 3:5-6 Isaiah 40:28-31 Jeremiah 17:5-8 1 Corinthians 1:26-31 SOAP Proverbs 3:5-6	Job 12:12 Psalm 92:12-14 1 Timothy 4:12 SOAP Psalm 92:12-14 1 Timothy 4:12
4	Isaiah 43:1-7 Matthew 5:16 1 Corinthians 10:31 SOAP Isaiah 43:7	2 Corinthians 12:9-10 1 Peter 2:9-10 SOAP 1 Peter 2:9-10	Proverbs 16:18 John 15:5 James 1:17 SOAP John 15:5	2 Corinthians 3:4-5 SOAP 2 Corinthians 3:4-5	Genesis 50:19-21 Isaiah 43:18-19 Philippians 1:12-14 1 Peter 2:22-23 SOAP Isaiah 43:18-19
5	Ecclesiastes 5:10 Hebrews 13:5 SOAP Hebrews 13:5	Ecclesiastes 3:11 Matthew 6:19-21 Luke 12:15 SOAP Matthew 6:19-21	Psalm 39:4 Proverbs 31:30 2 Corinthians 4:16-18 SOAP 2 Corinthians 4:16-18	Romans 5:3-5 James 1:2-4 1 Peter 4:12-13 SOAP James 1:2-4	Psalm 4:6-7 Psalm 68:3 Psalm 144:15 Psalm 146:5 SOAP Psalm 4:6-7
6	Ephesians 6:11-17 SOAP Ephesians 6:11	Proverbs 13:20 James 1:5 SOAP James 1:5	John 8:31-32 John 17:17 SOAP John 8:31-32	Psalm 25:5 Psalm 119:6 SOAP Psalm 25:5	Romans 12:2 Philippians 4:8 SOAP Philippians 4:8

Reflect

- *What does this passage reveal about the character of God?*

- *What does this passage reveal about the plan of God?*

- *What does this passage reveal about the heart and character of humanity?*

- *How does this passage reveal God's heart for His people?*

- *What have I learned about myself through this reading?*

- *What is God asking me to do with the truth I have learned?*

- *How can I share this with a friend today?*

- *Which promises of God do I need to remember as I go about my day?*

PRAYER REQUEST

GOD'S RESPONSE

PRAYER REQUEST

GOD'S RESPONSE

PRAYER REQUEST

GOD'S RESPONSE

TIME WITH HIM

READ	SOAP

SCRIPTURE / *Write the SOAP passage.*

OBSERVATION / *Write 3 or 4 observations.*

APPLICATION / *Write 1 or 2 applications.*

PRAYER / *Write a prayer over what you learned.*

TIME WITH HIM

READ	SOAP

SCRIPTURE / *Write the SOAP passage.*

_____
_____
_____
_____
_____
_____
_____
_____
_____
_____
_____
_____

OBSERVATION / *Write 3 or 4 observations.*

_____
_____
_____
_____
_____
_____
_____
_____
_____

APPLICATION / *Write 1 or 2 applications.*

PRAYER / *Write a prayer over what you learned.*

TIME WITH HIM

READ	SOAP

SCRIPTURE / *Write the SOAP passage.*

_____

_____

_____

_____

_____

_____

_____

_____

_____

_____

_____

_____

_____

_____

OBSERVATION / *Write 3 or 4 observations.*

_____

_____

_____

_____

_____

_____

_____

_____

APPLICATION / *Write 1 or 2 applications.*

PRAYER / *Write a prayer over what you learned.*

READ

SOAP

SCRIPTURE / *Write the SOAP passage.*

OBSERVATION / *Write 3 or 4 observations.*

APPLICATION / *Write 1 or 2 applications.*

PRAYER / *Write a prayer over what you learned.*

TIME WITH HIM

READ

SOAP

SCRIPTURE / *Write the SOAP passage.*

OBSERVATION / *Write 3 or 4 observations.*

APPLICATION / *Write 1 or 2 applications.*

PRAYER / *Write a prayer over what you learned.*

TIME WITH HIM

READ

SOAP

SCRIPTURE / *Write the SOAP passage.*

OBSERVATION / *Write 3 or 4 observations.*

APPLICATION / *Write 1 or 2 applications.*

PRAYER / *Write a prayer over what you learned.*

READ	SOAP

SCRIPTURE / *Write the SOAP passage.*

_____

_____

_____

_____

_____

_____

_____

_____

_____

_____

_____

_____

_____

OBSERVATION / *Write 3 or 4 observations.*

_____

_____

_____

_____

_____

_____

_____

_____

_____

_____

APPLICATION / *Write 1 or 2 applications.*

PRAYER / *Write a prayer over what you learned.*

TIME WITH HIM

READ

SOAP

SCRIPTURE / *Write the SOAP passage.*

OBSERVATION / *Write 3 or 4 observations.*

APPLICATION / *Write 1 or 2 applications.*

PRAYER / *Write a prayer over what you learned.*

TIME WITH HIM

READ

SOAP

SCRIPTURE / *Write the SOAP passage.*

OBSERVATION / *Write 3 or 4 observations.*

APPLICATION / *Write 1 or 2 applications.*

PRAYER / *Write a prayer over what you learned.*

TIME WITH HIM

READ

SOAP

SCRIPTURE / *Write the SOAP passage.*

OBSERVATION / *Write 3 or 4 observations.*

APPLICATION / *Write 1 or 2 applications.*

PRAYER / *Write a prayer over what you learned.*

TIME WITH HIM

READ

SOAP

SCRIPTURE / *Write the SOAP passage.*

OBSERVATION / *Write 3 or 4 observations.*

APPLICATION / *Write 1 or 2 applications.*

PRAYER / *Write a prayer over what you learned.*

READ	SOAP

SCRIPTURE / *Write the SOAP passage.*

_____

_____

_____

_____

_____

_____

_____

_____

_____

_____

_____

OBSERVATION / *Write 3 or 4 observations.*

_____

_____

_____

_____

_____

_____

_____

_____

APPLICATION / *Write 1 or 2 applications.*

PRAYER / *Write a prayer over what you learned.*

READ

SOAP

SCRIPTURE / *Write the SOAP passage.*

OBSERVATION / *Write 3 or 4 observations.*

APPLICATION / *Write 1 or 2 applications.*

PRAYER / *Write a prayer over what you learned.*

TIME WITH HIM

READ

SOAP

SCRIPTURE / *Write the SOAP passage.*

OBSERVATION / *Write 3 or 4 observations.*

APPLICATION / *Write 1 or 2 applications.*

PRAYER / *Write a prayer over what you learned.*

READ

SOAP

SCRIPTURE / *Write the SOAP passage.*

OBSERVATION / *Write 3 or 4 observations.*

APPLICATION / *Write 1 or 2 applications.*

PRAYER / *Write a prayer over what you learned.*

READ	SOAP

SCRIPTURE / *Write the SOAP passage.*

_____
_____
_____
_____
_____
_____
_____
_____
_____
_____
_____
_____

OBSERVATION / *Write 3 or 4 observations.*

_____
_____
_____
_____
_____
_____
_____
_____
_____

APPLICATION / *Write 1 or 2 applications.*

PRAYER / *Write a prayer over what you learned.*

TIME WITH HIM

READ	SOAP

SCRIPTURE / *Write the SOAP passage.*

OBSERVATION / *Write 3 or 4 observations.*

APPLICATION / *Write 1 or 2 applications.*

PRAYER / *Write a prayer over what you learned.*

TIME WITH HIM

READ	SOAP

SCRIPTURE / *Write the SOAP passage.*

OBSERVATION / *Write 3 or 4 observations.*

APPLICATION / *Write 1 or 2 applications.*

PRAYER / *Write a prayer over what you learned.*

TIME WITH HIM

READ	SOAP

SCRIPTURE / *Write the SOAP passage.*

OBSERVATION / *Write 3 or 4 observations.*

APPLICATION / *Write 1 or 2 applications.*

PRAYER / *Write a prayer over what you learned.*

TIME WITH HIM

READER

SOAP

SCRIPTURE / *Write the SOAP passage.*

_____

_____

_____

_____

_____

_____

_____

_____

_____

_____

_____

OBSERVATION / *Write 3 or 4 observations.*

_____

_____

_____

_____

_____

_____

_____

_____

APPLICATION / *Write 1 or 2 applications.*

PRAYER / *Write a prayer over what you learned.*

READ

SOAP

SCRIPTURE / *Write the SOAP passage.*

OBSERVATION / *Write 3 or 4 observations.*

APPLICATION / *Write 1 or 2 applications.*

PRAYER / *Write a prayer over what you learned.*

READ

SOAP

SCRIPTURE / *Write the SOAP passage.*

OBSERVATION / *Write 3 or 4 observations.*

APPLICATION / *Write 1 or 2 applications.*

PRAYER / *Write a prayer over what you learned.*

READ

SOAP

SCRIPTURE / *Write the SOAP passage.*

OBSERVATION / *Write 3 or 4 observations.*

APPLICATION / *Write 1 or 2 applications.*

PRAYER / *Write a prayer over what you learned.*

TIME WITH HIM

READ

SOAP

SCRIPTURE / *Write the SOAP passage.*

OBSERVATION / *Write 3 or 4 observations.*

APPLICATION / *Write 1 or 2 applications.*

PRAYER / *Write a prayer over what you learned.*

TIME WITH HIM

READn | SOAP

SCRIPTURE / *Write the SOAP passage.*

OBSERVATION / *Write 3 or 4 observations.*

APPLICATION / *Write 1 or 2 applications.*

PRAYER / *Write a prayer over what you learned.*

TIME WITH HIM

READ

SOAP

SCRIPTURE / *Write the SOAP passage.*

_____
_____
_____
_____
_____
_____
_____
_____
_____
_____
_____
_____

OBSERVATION / *Write 3 or 4 observations.*

_____
_____
_____
_____
_____
_____
_____
_____
_____

APPLICATION / *Write 1 or 2 applications.*

PRAYER / *Write a prayer over what you learned.*

TIME WITH HIM

READ

SOAP

SCRIPTURE / *Write the SOAP passage.*

OBSERVATION / *Write 3 or 4 observations.*

APPLICATION / *Write 1 or 2 applications.*

PRAYER / *Write a prayer over what you learned.*

TIME WITH HIM

READ

SOAP

SCRIPTURE / *Write the SOAP passage.*

OBSERVATION / *Write 3 or 4 observations.*

APPLICATION / *Write 1 or 2 applications.*

PRAYER / *Write a prayer over what you learned.*

TIME WITH HIM

READ

SOAP

SCRIPTURE / *Write the SOAP passage.*

OBSERVATION / *Write 3 or 4 observations.*

APPLICATION / *Write 1 or 2 applications.*

PRAYER / *Write a prayer over what you learned.*

TIME WITH HIM

READ

SOAP

SCRIPTURE / *Write the SOAP passage.*

OBSERVATION / *Write 3 or 4 observations.*

APPLICATION / *Write 1 or 2 applications.*

PRAYER / *Write a prayer over what you learned.*

TIME WITH HIM

READ

SOAP

SCRIPTURE / *Write the SOAP passage.*

_____
_____
_____
_____
_____
_____
_____
_____
_____
_____
_____
_____

OBSERVATION / *Write 3 or 4 observations.*

_____
_____
_____
_____
_____
_____
_____
_____
_____
_____

APPLICATION / *Write 1 or 2 applications.*

PRAYER / *Write a prayer over what you learned.*

READ

SOAP

SCRIPTURE / *Write the SOAP passage.*

OBSERVATION / *Write 3 or 4 observations.*

APPLICATION / *Write 1 or 2 applications.*

PRAYER / *Write a prayer over what you learned.*

READ

SOAP

SCRIPTURE / *Write the SOAP passage.*

OBSERVATION / *Write 3 or 4 observations.*

APPLICATION / *Write 1 or 2 applications.*

PRAYER / *Write a prayer over what you learned.*

TIME WITH HIM

READ	SOAP

SCRIPTURE / *Write the SOAP passage.*

OBSERVATION / *Write 3 or 4 observations.*

APPLICATION / *Write 1 or 2 applications.*

PRAYER / *Write a prayer over what you learned.*

TIME WITH HIM

READ	SOAP

SCRIPTURE / *Write the SOAP passage.*

OBSERVATION / *Write 3 or 4 observations.*

APPLICATION / *Write 1 or 2 applications.*

PRAYER / *Write a prayer over what you learned.*

READ	SOAP

SCRIPTURE / *Write the SOAP passage.*

OBSERVATION / *Write 3 or 4 observations.*

APPLICATION / *Write 1 or 2 applications.*

PRAYER / *Write a prayer over what you learned.*

TIME WITH HIM

READ

SOAP

SCRIPTURE / *Write the SOAP passage.*

OBSERVATION / *Write 3 or 4 observations.*

APPLICATION / *Write 1 or 2 applications.*

PRAYER / *Write a prayer over what you learned.*

TIME WITH HIM

READ	SOAP

SCRIPTURE / *Write the SOAP passage.*

OBSERVATION / *Write 3 or 4 observations.*

APPLICATION / *Write 1 or 2 applications.*

PRAYER / *Write a prayer over what you learned.*

READ

SOAP

SCRIPTURE / *Write the SOAP passage.*

OBSERVATION / *Write 3 or 4 observations.*

APPLICATION / *Write 1 or 2 applications.*

PRAYER / *Write a prayer over what you learned.*

TIME WITH HIM

READ

SOAP

SCRIPTURE / *Write the SOAP passage.*

OBSERVATION / *Write 3 or 4 observations.*

APPLICATION / *Write 1 or 2 applications.*

PRAYER / *Write a prayer over what you learned.*

READ

SOAP

SCRIPTURE / *Write the SOAP passage.*

OBSERVATION / *Write 3 or 4 observations.*

APPLICATION / *Write 1 or 2 applications.*

PRAYER / *Write a prayer over what you learned.*

TIME WITH HIM

READ

SOAP

SCRIPTURE / *Write the SOAP passage.*

OBSERVATION / *Write 3 or 4 observations.*

APPLICATION / *Write 1 or 2 applications.*

PRAYER / *Write a prayer over what you learned.*

READ

SOAP

SCRIPTURE / *Write the SOAP passage.*

OBSERVATION / *Write 3 or 4 observations.*

APPLICATION / *Write 1 or 2 applications.*

PRAYER / *Write a prayer over what you learned.*

TIME WITH HIM

READ | SOAP

SCRIPTURE / *Write the SOAP passage.*

OBSERVATION / *Write 3 or 4 observations.*

APPLICATION / *Write 1 or 2 applications.*

PRAYER / *Write a prayer over what you learned.*

TIME WITH HIM

READ

SOAP

SCRIPTURE / *Write the SOAP passage.*

OBSERVATION / *Write 3 or 4 observations.*

APPLICATION / *Write 1 or 2 applications.*

PRAYER / *Write a prayer over what you learned.*

READ

SOAP

SCRIPTURE / *Write the SOAP passage.*

OBSERVATION / *Write 3 or 4 observations.*

APPLICATION / *Write 1 or 2 applications.*

PRAYER / *Write a prayer over what you learned.*

TIME WITH HIM

READ

SOAP

SCRIPTURE / *Write the SOAP passage.*

OBSERVATION / *Write 3 or 4 observations.*

APPLICATION / *Write 1 or 2 applications.*

PRAYER / *Write a prayer over what you learned.*

TIME WITH HIM

READ

SOAP

SCRIPTURE / *Write the SOAP passage.*

OBSERVATION / *Write 3 or 4 observations.*

APPLICATION / *Write 1 or 2 applications.*

PRAYER / *Write a prayer over what you learned.*

TIME WITH HIM

READ

SOAP

SCRIPTURE / *Write the SOAP passage.*

OBSERVATION / *Write 3 or 4 observations.*

APPLICATION / *Write 1 or 2 applications.*

PRAYER / *Write a prayer over what you learned.*

TIME WITH HIM

READ

SOAP

SCRIPTURE / *Write the SOAP passage.*

OBSERVATION / *Write 3 or 4 observations.*

APPLICATION / *Write 1 or 2 applications.*

PRAYER / *Write a prayer over what you learned.*

TIME WITH HIM

READ

SOAP

SCRIPTURE / *Write the SOAP passage.*

OBSERVATION / *Write 3 or 4 observations.*

APPLICATION / *Write 1 or 2 applications.*

PRAYER / *Write a prayer over what you learned.*

TIME WITH HIM

READ	SOAP

SCRIPTURE / *Write the SOAP passage.*

_____

_____

_____

_____

_____

_____

_____

_____

_____

_____

_____

OBSERVATION / *Write 3 or 4 observations.*

_____

_____

_____

_____

_____

_____

_____

APPLICATION / *Write 1 or 2 applications.*

PRAYER / *Write a prayer over what you learned.*

READ

SOAP

SCRIPTURE / *Write the SOAP passage.*

OBSERVATION / *Write 3 or 4 observations.*

APPLICATION / *Write 1 or 2 applications.*

PRAYER / *Write a prayer over what you learned.*

TIME WITH HIM

READ

SOAP

SCRIPTURE / *Write the SOAP passage.*

OBSERVATION / *Write 3 or 4 observations.*

APPLICATION / *Write 1 or 2 applications.*

PRAYER / *Write a prayer over what you learned.*

READ	SOAP

SCRIPTURE / *Write the SOAP passage.*

OBSERVATION / *Write 3 or 4 observations.*

APPLICATION / *Write 1 or 2 applications.*

PRAYER / *Write a prayer over what you learned.*

TIME WITH HIM

READ

SOAP

SCRIPTURE / *Write the SOAP passage.*

OBSERVATION / *Write 3 or 4 observations.*

APPLICATION / *Write 1 or 2 applications.*

PRAYER / *Write a prayer over what you learned.*

TIME WITH HIM

READ	SOAP

SCRIPTURE / *Write the SOAP passage.*

OBSERVATION / *Write 3 or 4 observations.*

APPLICATION / *Write 1 or 2 applications.*

PRAYER / *Write a prayer over what you learned.*

TIME WITH HIM

READ | SOAP

SCRIPTURE / *Write the SOAP passage.*

OBSERVATION / *Write 3 or 4 observations.*

APPLICATION / *Write 1 or 2 applications.*

PRAYER / *Write a prayer over what you learned.*

TIME WITH HIM

READ

SOAP

SCRIPTURE / *Write the SOAP passage.*

OBSERVATION / *Write 3 or 4 observations.*

APPLICATION / *Write 1 or 2 applications.*

PRAYER / *Write a prayer over what you learned.*

TIME WITH HIM

READ	SOAP

SCRIPTURE / *Write the SOAP passage.*

OBSERVATION / *Write 3 or 4 observations.*

APPLICATION / *Write 1 or 2 applications.*

PRAYER / *Write a prayer over what you learned.*

TIME WITH HIM

READ	SOAP

SCRIPTURE / *Write the SOAP passage.*

OBSERVATION / *Write 3 or 4 observations.*

APPLICATION / *Write 1 or 2 applications.*

PRAYER / *Write a prayer over what you learned.*

TIME WITH HIM

READ

SOAP

SCRIPTURE / *Write the SOAP passage.*

OBSERVATION / *Write 3 or 4 observations.*

APPLICATION / *Write 1 or 2 applications.*

PRAYER / *Write a prayer over what you learned.*

TIME WITH HIM

READ	SOAP

SCRIPTURE / *Write the SOAP passage.*

OBSERVATION / *Write 3 or 4 observations.*

APPLICATION / *Write 1 or 2 applications.*

PRAYER / *Write a prayer over what you learned.*

READ

SOAP

SCRIPTURE / *Write the SOAP passage.*

OBSERVATION / *Write 3 or 4 observations.*

APPLICATION / *Write 1 or 2 applications.*

PRAYER / *Write a prayer over what you learned.*

TIME WITH HIM

READ	SOAP

SCRIPTURE / *Write the SOAP passage.*

OBSERVATION / *Write 3 or 4 observations.*

TIME WITH HIM

READ	SOAP

SCRIPTURE / *Write the SOAP passage.*

OBSERVATION / *Write 3 or 4 observations.*

APPLICATION / *Write 1 or 2 applications.*

PRAYER / *Write a prayer over what you learned.*

TIME WITH HIM

READ

SOAP

SCRIPTURE / *Write the SOAP passage.*

OBSERVATION / *Write 3 or 4 observations.*

APPLICATION / *Write 1 or 2 applications.*

PRAYER / *Write a prayer over what you learned.*

TIME WITH HIM

READ

SOAP

SCRIPTURE / *Write the SOAP passage.*

OBSERVATION / *Write 3 or 4 observations.*

PRAYER / *Write a prayer over what you learned.*

READ

SOAP

SCRIPTURE / *Write the SOAP passage.*

OBSERVATION / *Write 3 or 4 observations.*

APPLICATION / *Write 1 or 2 applications.*

PRAYER / *Write a prayer over what you learned.*

TIME WITH HIM

READ

SOAP

SCRIPTURE / *Write the SOAP passage.*

OBSERVATION / *Write 3 or 4 observations.*

APPLICATION / *Write 1 or 2 applications.*

PRAYER / *Write a prayer over what you learned.*

TIME WITH HIM

READ

SOAP

SCRIPTURE / *Write the SOAP passage.*

OBSERVATION / *Write 3 or 4 observations.*

APPLICATION / *Write 1 or 2 applications.*

PRAYER / *Write a prayer over what you learned.*

TIME WITH HIM

READ	SOAP

SCRIPTURE / *Write the SOAP passage.*

OBSERVATION / *Write 3 or 4 observations.*

APPLICATION / *Write 1 or 2 applications.*

PRAYER / *Write a prayer over what you learned.*

TIME WITH HIM

READ	SOAP

SCRIPTURE / *Write the SOAP passage.*

OBSERVATION / *Write 3 or 4 observations.*

APPLICATION / *Write 1 or 2 applications.*

PRAYER / *Write a prayer over what you learned.*

TIME WITH HIM

READ

SOAP

SCRIPTURE / *Write the SOAP passage.*

OBSERVATION / *Write 3 or 4 observations.*

APPLICATION / *Write 1 or 2 applications.*

PRAYER / *Write a prayer over what you learned.*

READ

SOAP

SCRIPTURE / *Write the SOAP passage.*

OBSERVATION / *Write 3 or 4 observations.*

APPLICATION / *Write 1 or 2 applications.*

PRAYER / *Write a prayer over what you learned.*

TIME WITH HIM

READ

SOAP

SCRIPTURE / *Write the SOAP passage.*

OBSERVATION / *Write 3 or 4 observations.*

APPLICATION / *Write 1 or 2 applications.*

PRAYER / *Write a prayer over what you learned.*

TIME WITH HIM

READ	SOAP

SCRIPTURE / *Write the SOAP passage.*

OBSERVATION / *Write 3 or 4 observations.*

APPLICATION / *Write 1 or 2 applications.*

PRAYER / *Write a prayer over what you learned.*

TIME WITH HIM

READ	SOAP

SCRIPTURE / *Write the SOAP passage.*

OBSERVATION / *Write 3 or 4 observations.*

APPLICATION / *Write 1 or 2 applications.*

PRAYER / *Write a prayer over what you learned.*

READ

SOAP

SCRIPTURE / *Write the SOAP passage.*

OBSERVATION / *Write 3 or 4 observations.*

APPLICATION / *Write 1 or 2 applications.*

PRAYER / *Write a prayer over what you learned.*

TIME WITH HIM

READ

SOAP

SCRIPTURE / *Write the SOAP passage.*

OBSERVATION / *Write 3 or 4 observations.*

APPLICATION / *Write 1 or 2 applications.*

PRAYER / *Write a prayer over what you learned.*

TIME WITH HIM

READ	SOAP

SCRIPTURE / *Write the SOAP passage.*

OBSERVATION / *Write 3 or 4 observations.*

APPLICATION / *Write 1 or 2 applications.*

PRAYER / *Write a prayer over what you learned.*

TIME WITH HIM

READ	SOAP

SCRIPTURE / *Write the SOAP passage.*

OBSERVATION / *Write 3 or 4 observations.*

APPLICATION / *Write 1 or 2 applications.*

PRAYER / *Write a prayer over what you learned.*

READ

SOAP

SCRIPTURE / *Write the SOAP passage.*

OBSERVATION / *Write 3 or 4 observations.*

APPLICATION / *Write 1 or 2 applications.*

PRAYER / *Write a prayer over what you learned.*

TIME WITH HIM

READ	SOAP

SCRIPTURE / *Write the SOAP passage.*

OBSERVATION / *Write 3 or 4 observations.*

APPLICATION / *Write 1 or 2 applications.*

PRAYER / *Write a prayer over what you learned.*

READ

SOAP

SCRIPTURE / *Write the SOAP passage.*

OBSERVATION / *Write 3 or 4 observations.*

APPLICATION / *Write 1 or 2 applications.*

PRAYER / *Write a prayer over what you learned.*

TIME WITH HIM

READ	SOAP

SCRIPTURE / *Write the SOAP passage.*

OBSERVATION / *Write 3 or 4 observations.*

APPLICATION / *Write 1 or 2 applications.*

PRAYER / *Write a prayer over what you learned.*

READ

SOAP

SCRIPTURE / *Write the SOAP passage.*

OBSERVATION / *Write 3 or 4 observations.*

APPLICATION / *Write 1 or 2 applications.*

PRAYER / *Write a prayer over what you learned.*

TIME WITH HIM

READ	SOAP

SCRIPTURE / *Write the SOAP passage.*

OBSERVATION / *Write 3 or 4 observations.*

APPLICATION / *Write 1 or 2 applications.*

PRAYER / *Write a prayer over what you learned.*

TIME WITH HIM

READ

SOAP

SCRIPTURE / *Write the SOAP passage.*

OBSERVATION / *Write 3 or 4 observations.*

APPLICATION / *Write 1 or 2 applications.*

PRAYER / *Write a prayer over what you learned.*

TIME WITH HIM

READ

SOAP

SCRIPTURE / *Write the SOAP passage.*

OBSERVATION / *Write 3 or 4 observations.*

APPLICATION / *Write 1 or 2 applications.*

PRAYER / *Write a prayer over what you learned.*

TIME WITH HIM

READ	SOAP

SCRIPTURE / *Write the SOAP passage.*

OBSERVATION / *Write 3 or 4 observations.*

APPLICATION / *Write 1 or 2 applications.*

PRAYER / *Write a prayer over what you learned.*

TIME WITH HIM

SCRIPTURE / *Write the SOAP passage.*

OBSERVATION / *Write 3 or 4 observations.*

APPLICATION / *Write 1 or 2 applications.*

PRAYER / *Write a prayer over what you learned.*

TIME WITH HIM

READ

SOAP

SCRIPTURE / *Write the SOAP passage.*

OBSERVATION / *Write 3 or 4 observations.*

/ *Write 1 or 2 applications.*

/ *Write a prayer over what you learned.*

READ	SOAP

SCRIPTURE / *Write the SOAP passage.*

OBSERVATION / *Write 3 or 4 observations.*

APPLICATION / *Write 1 or 2 applications.*

PRAYER / *Write a prayer over what you learned.*

READ

SOAP

;

SCRIPTURE / *Write the SOAP passage.*

OBSERVATION / *Write 3 or 4 observations.*

APPLICATION / *Write 1 or 2 applications.*

PRAYER / *Write a prayer over what you learned.*

TIME WITH HIM

READ

SOAP

SCRIPTURE / *Write the SOAP passage.*

OBSERVATION / *Write 3 or 4 observations.*

APPLICATION / *Write 1 or 2 applications.*

PRAYER / *Write a prayer over what you learned.*

TIME WITH HIM

READ | SOAP

SCRIPTURE / *Write the SOAP passage.*

OBSERVATION / *Write 3 or 4 observations.*

APPLICATION / *Write 1 or 2 applications.*

PRAYER / *Write a prayer over what you learned.*

THE One WHO testifies TO THESE THINGS says, "Yes, I AM COMING SOON!" Amen! Come, Lord Jesus!

S / SCRIPTURE

God's Word is living and active (see Heb 4:12). Studying God's Word is valuable and important for our lives, but so is memorizing it. When we memorize and meditate on God's Word we are able to bring it to mind in many types of situations: trials, temptations, sadness, pain, joy, and celebration.

The first stage of the SOAP method is Scripture. Here, we take time to write out the verse or verses in full. This helps us memorize and internalize God's Word. In Colossians 3:16 we are told to "let the word of Christ dwell in you richly." To dwell means to live; we are to let God's Word live in us. In order to do this, we need to study it deeply and commit it to memory.

If our hearts are filled with God's Word, then we will speak of Him more often. He will be in the conversations we have and the things we do.

Jesus quoted Scripture all the time, showing that He took the time to memorize it. During Jesus' temptation in the desert He proclaimed the truth of Scripture to combat the attacks of the enemy. If Jesus memorized Scripture, then we definitely need to memorize Scripture! Sure, we can open our Bible and read verses, but how much more battle ready would we be if we could recall verses from memory without having to look them up?

Matthew 12:34 says, "For the mouth speaks from what fills the heart." What comes out of our mouths? Complaining? Anger? Pessimism? These are signs that the Word of God does not dwell in us richly, because what is in our hearts comes out of our mouths. If our hearts are filled with God's Word, then we will speak of Him more often. He will be in the conversations we have and the things we do. He will influence the way we talk about our circumstances and the way we talk about others.

Like Bible study, Scripture memorization takes work and time. There are no shortcuts. It is worth the work. As we study God's Word, taking time to memorize His Word is something that will enhance our study of Scripture as well as our lives.

Observation is a critical aspect of Bible study. It not only forces us to look at the text carefully, but it also helps us slow down and examine what is happening in the passage. The more time we spend observing a passage, the more accurate our interpretation and application of the passage will be. However, if we rush through observation, we are more prone to make mistakes in our interpretation and application later on.

An observation is taking note of something you see. When you observe the world around you, you do so with your five senses: sight, smell, taste, hearing, and touch. When reading the Bible only one of those senses, the sense of sight, is engaged.

A key element of observation is sticking with observation. It takes a great deal of discipline and practice not to jump to conclusions, interpretations, and applications when observing a passage. Observation asks and answers only one question: "What do I see?" You may be able to come to a reasonable conclusion regarding what the verse is saying, but that is not the practice of observation.

HERE ARE SOME ADDITIONAL QUESTIONS TO ASK DURING
OBSERVATION THAT WILL HELP ANSWER THE QUESTION
"WHAT DO I SEE?"

- *Who is talking?*
- *To whom are they speaking?*
- *What are they saying?*
- *What is the meaning of this word?*
- *What action is accomplished or implied?*
- *How is the action accomplished?*
- *Which literary devices are used?*
- *Are there any repeated words or phrases?*
- *Is anything unclear?*

- *Is there an element of time?*
- *Are the events listed sequentially?*
- *Are there any repeated words or phrases?*
- *Are there any key words?*
- *Who are the key players in the passage?*
- *Are there any explanations?*
- *Are there any comparisons?*
- *Which verbs are used?*
- *Which other parts of speech are present?*

THE PENTATEUCH: Genesis, Exodus, Leviticus, Numbers, and Deuteronomy form what is called the Pentateuch. The Pentateuch contains several genres, including historical accounts, codes of law, and poetry. When reading these books, we read the historical records as true events that occurred to real people. We learn a great deal about God, His character, and the way He interacts with humanity.

HISTORICAL BOOKS: Both the Old and New Testaments contain historical books. Joshua, Judges, Ruth, 1 and 2 Samuel, 1 and 2 Kings, 1 and 2 Chronicles, Ezra, Nehemiah, and Esther make up the historical section in the Old Testament. In the New Testament, the Book of Acts contains the historical record of the early church. These books were written by a variety of different authors to a variety of different audiences. The accounts contained in the historical books are also real events that happened to real people.

POETIC BOOKS: Job, Psalms, Proverbs, Ecclesiastes, and Song of Solomon are considered books of poetry. Each of these books contains a host of literary devices like similes, metaphors, repetition, allegory, hyperbole, and exaggeration. We can learn a great deal from these authors about how to understand and express emotion, how to ask God questions, how to deal with pain and loss, how to rejoice and offer praise, and how to live a faithful life.

PROPHETS: Isaiah, Jeremiah, Lamentations, Ezekiel, and Daniel are called the Major Prophets while Hosea, Joel, Amos, Obadiah, Jonah, Micah, Nahum, Habakkuk, Zephaniah, Haggai, Zechariah, and Malachi are considered the Minor Prophets. While these promises were not written to us, they tell us a great deal about God's character. They tell us what God loves and what God hates, what He honors, and what He punishes.

GOSPELS: The first four books of the New Testament are the accounts of Jesus' incarnation. The word *Gospel* comes from the Greek word for "good news." Matthew, Mark, Luke, and John each tell of the good news of Jesus Christ, of His life, death, and resurrection. Each of the Gospels is written from a different perspective, and each Gospel highlights a different aspect of Jesus' life and His ministry.

EPISTLES: Romans, 1 and 2 Corinthians, Galatians, Ephesians, Philippians, Colossians, 1 and 2 Thessalonians, 1 and 2 Timothy, Titus, Philemon, Hebrews, James, 1 and 2 Peter, 1, 2, and 3 John, and Jude are called epistles. When reading an epistle, it is important to have an overall understanding of the main message of the letter. Taking extra time to study the cultural and historical background of the letter will prove to be invaluable for understanding the context and meaning of the letter.

APOCALYPTIC: The New Testament also contains a prophetic book. The Book of Revelation is a message of prophecy regarding the end times and the second coming of Christ. The way we read Revelation is unique to other books of the Bible. While we find many words of judgment, we also find words of promise and redemption. We can find hope in the promise of Christ's return and of our eternity with Him.

Interpretation seeks to determine the author's intended meaning for his original audience. The question should never be, "What does this passage mean to you?"

Scripture was written for a specific audience, in a specific time and culture. In order to determine the theological meaning and emphasis of a passage accurately, we must take these things into account. What we think a passage means to us is irrelevant, and frankly, dangerous. In interpretation, our goal is to determine the theological truth of the passage—an unchanging and timeless truth that applies to all cultures and all peoples.

AS WE SEEK TO DISCERN THE AUTHOR'S INTENDED MEANING FOR THE ORIGINAL AUDIENCE, WE SHOULD KEEP IN MIND THE FOLLOWING:

- *Avoid reading our current culture and circumstances into the text.*
- *Assume a normal use of language; don't look for hidden meanings in the text.*
- *Keep in mind the overall context and story of the book.*
- *Allow clear passages to illuminate difficult passages; don't seek to redefine a clear passage by interpreting a difficult passage.*
- *Research and understand the historical and cultural background.*
- *Look up difficult words or phrases.*

INTERPRETIVE QUESTIONS TO ASK ABOUT A PASSAGE:

- *Who is the speaker?*
- *Who is the intended audience?*
- *What do we know about the audience?*
- *In which time period did the events take place?*
- *What issues does the speaker address?*
- *Are any of the ideas expressed repeated elsewhere in the Bible? If so, where?*
- *Does the speaker give any commands or prohibitions in the passage?*
- *Does the speaker explain why he commands the audience to do (or not do) something?*
- *What insight do the surrounding verses provide into the meaning of this verse?*
- *What is the overall context of the passage in which the verse is found?*

Keep in mind in order to answer these questions, additional resources may be needed. A good study Bible and Bible commentaries are excellent resources to help us determine the cultural and historical context of a passage. Surrounding passages and verses can also help us answer these questions.

SIMILE

A simile is a form of comparison between two things or ideas. It makes an explicit comparison and is linked by the words *like* or *as*.
Ex: Psalm 1:3 "He is like a tree planted by flowing streams."

METAPHOR

A metaphor is another form of comparison between two things. The comparison states that something—one thing—is another thing.
Ex: Psalm 23:1 "The LORD is my shepherd."

PERSONIFICATION

Personification is a form of representation in which an inanimate object is given human characteristics or qualities.
Ex: Joel 1:10 "The ground is in mourning."

ANTHROPOMORPHISM

God, who is invisible and immaterial, is often represented with human characteristics. An anthropomorphism represents God as human.
Ex: Psalm 138:7 "Your right hand delivers me."

SYMBOLISM

Symbolism uses a material, physical object to represent a spiritual or moral truth. Sometimes these are explicitly stated in the text, and other times they are implied.
Ex: Deuteronomy 16:3 "For seven days you must eat bread made without yeast, as symbolic of affliction."

HYPERBOLE

Hyperbole is an intentional exaggeration made in order to emphasize a point.
Ex: Matthew 19:24 "It is easier for a camel to go through the eye of a needle than for a rich person to enter into the kingdom of God."

IRONY

Irony involves the use of language contrary to the actual meaning he or she intends to convey. It typically comes in the form of sarcasm or mockery.
Ex: 2 Samuel 6:20 "How the king of Israel has distinguished himself this day!"

REPETITION

Repetition involves repeating the same words or phrases in order to make a point or emphasize an idea.
Ex: Isaiah 26:3 "You will keep in peace peace" (This is not conveyed in many English translations, but the Hebrew word shalom is repeated for emphasis.)

RHETORICAL QUESTION

When an author uses a rhetorical question, he is not looking for an answer to his question. Rather, he is making an argument by posing the question.
Ex: Job 39:1 "Are you acquainted with the way the mountain goats give birth?"

Gordon Johnston, "Interpretation of Biblical Hebrew Poetry—5," Introduction to Biblical Hebrew Poetry, Dallas Theological Seminary, Dallas, TX, January 31, 2019.

Application is an important part of studying our Bibles. It is how we take what we have learned and put it into practice in our lives. We first have to be sure that we have a proper understanding of what the text is teaching so that our application is right and honoring to the Lord.

The goal of application is to find key principles that are relevant in our current context. A principle is an outstanding and abiding truth that is not limited by time or context.

DOES THE PASSAGE AND RELATED OBSERVATION AND INTERPRETATION REVEAL:

• *Something for which I should praise or thank God?*

• *A promise for me to claim or a truth for me to believe?*

• *Something I need to change or begin doing?*

• *Something or someone I need to pray for?*

• *A relationship I need to work on?*

• *A sin problem I need to address?*

WHAT OR HOW DOES THIS PASSAGE:

T – Teach

R – Reprove

C – Correct

I – Instruct

Don't skip over passages that don't clearly tell you about something you should be doing. Look for truths that will help you renew your mind and love God more.

As you determine applications, make them practical and actionable. While it is often encouraging to have applications such as "Trust God!" and "Love others!" these are often difficult to put into practice without specific ways to accomplish them. Possible alternatives would be "Give one hundred dollars a month to my church and trust that God will meet my financial needs" or "Spend one hour each week writing encouraging notes to three friends." Making our applications actionable and practical will help us see the fruit of God's Word grow in our lives.

Prayer is the final piece of the SOAP method. Here, we take what we have learned through observation and how we have determined to apply the passage to our lives through application, and we pray it back to God.

WHEN PRAYING THROUGH A PASSAGE, FIRST ANSWER
THESE QUESTIONS:

- *What does this passage tell me about God?*

- *According to what I have learned from this passage, what are some reasons to rejoice?*

- *What does this passage reveal that encourages me to make changes in my life?*

- *What request can I make in light of this passage?*

The answers to these questions become an outline for how to pray. First, we can praise God for who He is and what He does. Then, we can rejoice and thank Him for the truth of His Word and what He is doing in the world. Next, we can repent and ask God to change our hearts, free us from sin, or give us wisdom and discernment. Finally, we can bring our requests to God.